MANIFEST

GREATNESS

BY: SYLVESTER CHISOM

Sylvester Chisom
© 2017 Manifest Greatness Publishing

ISBN 978-0-692-99152-7

PRINTED IN THE UNITED STATES

FIRST EDITION: NOVERMBER 2017

For special quantity discounts for bulk purchases:

booking@sylvesterchisom.com

I wrote, "Manifest Greatness" with love for you.

You don't have to be great to get started.

But you have to get started to be great.

- Sylvester Chisom

CONTENTS

CONTENTS

Preface

The burning question is, what does it mean to manifest greatness? It means that you are living your truth, your purpose. It means you are giving all of yourself to the world. You are prepared to add value, lead, collaborate, and solve problems everywhere you go. It means you are not sitting on your gifts and talents. It means you are overcoming fear, self-doubt, and anger. It means you are living a life dedicated to helping others.

It means you are letting go of any comparisons to other people. Ultimately it means you are living life without limits!

I must warn you, this book may be a little dangerous because the principles discussed in, "Manifest Greatness" will make you rethink some areas of your life. This book is designed to challenge any limiting beliefs you have historically told yourself. It is dangerous because it is going to push you north of mediocre, north of good. You will push far north, which means we are aiming for greatness. "Manifest Greatness," is for you if you desire to excel. You will learn to apply the entrepreneurial mindset to your life. That means you will learn to take ownership of every aspect of your life. Manifesting Greatness is a lifestyle.

I wrote, "Manifest Greatness" to help you recalibrate, and incorporate positive disruption into your life. I firmly believe that we only grow through discomfort or insight, not from apathy. We do not grow from sitting back and doing nothing or being unaware.

That is why this book and lifestyle is dangerous because it will disrupt areas of your life. Ask yourself, "Is it my desire to have a breakthrough to a new level of success?" Would you like to know and apply the same strategies used to create success and impact by some of the most significant industry leaders, thought leaders, and humanitarians? These strategies have produced success for the likes of Steve Jobs, Aristotle, Dr. Dre, President Eisenhower, David Steward, Seth Godin, and so many more.

How would you feel if you achieved more greatness in your life? If you take action on these principles, you will become a better problem solver, innovator, and self-directed leader. *Manifest Greatness* will awaken something on the inside of you and offer you a new model for living. A 21st century model. Your journey to greatness begins now.

1

CARING

CONSCIOUSNESS

MANIFEST GREATNESS

THE ONLY WAY TO DO GREAT WORK IS TO LOVE WHAT YOU DO.

-STEVE JOBS-

MANIFESTGREATNESS.ORG

12

The first principle of manifesting greatness will focus on your intentions. The goal for you is to have everything you do come from a great place. Great intentions will lead to great thoughts, which will in turn lead to great actions. The caring consciousness is a principle aimed at getting you to let everything you do come from the heart.

Let your work come from the heart. Your conversations with people let it come from the heart. The way you approach connecting with others let it come from the heart. Your contributions to your family, your community, and to the world let it all come from a great place.

I was recently having a conversation with fellow content creator, Prince EA. He is a filmmaker, global change agent, and YouTube superstar. This man has over one billion views on Facebook and YouTube spreading a message of love, peace, respect for the Earth; he is an all-around humanitarian. So we were having a conversation about success, living well and ways we want to positively impact the world. One of the things I was curious about was how has he been so successful with spreading his message through YouTube videos.

I asked him what was his secret. I was curious to learn some new things that I could incorporate into my videos. Here I am excited about a few thousand views, and he has millions of views per video. So with great anticipation I am waiting to hear from him on what he is doing differently. I expected a technical answer and without giving it much thought he said, "I approach every video like it is my last and I let the message come from the heart." This was not the answer I was expecting at all. However, after I thought about what Prince EA said for a few days, I began to understand what he meant. By taking a moment to remind yourself to let your thoughts and actions about your work come from the heart, you project a higher level of authenticity to the world. The vibration is intangible; we cannot physically feel it. However, emotionally we can feel it when someone is applying the principle of the caring consciousness. Emotionally, other people will connect with you and your work on a deeper level. The caring consciousness is rooted in empathy and putting others first. Let all of your contributions to the world come from the heart. This is the starting point of manifesting greatness.

MANIFEST GREATNESS ASSESSMENT 1

CREATE A GOAL WITH MEANING

The practice of the caring consciousness involves being present with yourself and focusing on goals that have meaning to you and that impact others positively. Complete the Manifest Greatness Empathy Map as if you have achieved your goal. Write down your answers or get creative and draw pictures for your answers.

Write down a goal that you would like to achieve?

Why is it important to you?

Manifest Greatness Empathy Map

Feelings
How do you feel? How do other people feel?

Influences
What people, places, or things may influence your ability to achieve your goal?

Goal
Imagine you have accomplished your goal.

Senses
What do you hear? What do you see? What do you smell?

Impact
What problem do you solve by achieving this goal? How does achieving this goal help other people.

2

CONFIDENCE

CONFIDENCE IS THE BEST OUTFIT. ROCK IT! OWN IT!

MANIFESTGREATNESS.ORG

For you to manifest greatness, you will need to have supreme confidence and belief in yourself. For you to be the greatest leader you want to be certain about what you are using your gifts to create and your desire to positively impact others.

For the past three years I have had the fantastic opportunity to travel with social entrepreneur students to Costa Rica. I work with an extraordinary organization founded by Samantha Lurie in St. Louis, MO called, The Show Me Costa Rica Project. Over the past 5 years we have raised over $200,000 and taken 82 students from inner-city public schools to Costa Rica to study science and global culture. Many of the students are the first to travel internationally in their families. Each year we experience so many great firsts together that require confidence like hiking volcanoes, rain forests, and snorkeling on a coral reef. They learn things about why specific food products grow best in certain parts of the world.

For example, some of the best coffee in the world comes from Costa Rica due to the high elevations and the nutrient rich volcanic soil. Our students were so inspired by being on real coffee farms that they started a premium Costa Rican coffee business to pay for their educational trip. It is impressive to see how people respond to our students every week at farmers' markets and online when they know their coffee budget is now going to a good cause. For me it is one of the most fulfilling projects I have ever supported. It is an honor helping mentor students and raising money to support them.

I want to share a unique story as it relates to confidence from our time in a Costa Rican rainforest. As we were walking through the rainforest, I noticed a lot of beautiful tropical plants and wildlife. Most of these things you can only see in a rainforest. Beautiful butterflies, rare trees, and birds. There was one bird in particular that stood out to me. I noticed this beautiful quetzal with colorful feathers fly over our heads and land on a tree branch that was very high up. The bird stood tall, chest out with supreme confidence. I stood still and watched the bird for almost a minute. As the bird was resting there in the security of the branch on that tree, a massive gust of wind came through. We all felt the strong wind move us abruptly, so I know the bird had to feel the wind too. However, even after that strong gust of wind came through the bird did not budge.

The beautiful quetzal did not move because it was confident in the ability of its wings. The bird knew that if for some reason the branch failed or it was pushed off the branch, that she could fly. It is having that confidence in her abilities that led her to stand with supreme confidence in that moment.

I think in that short story there is a perfect example for all of us to know that we must have the confidence in our abilities, the confidence in our wings that we too can fly.

So as you approach your goals right now, you have to be certain that you have what it takes to get it done. You must believe in yourself. You truly have to believe in yourself. I want you right now, just to take a deep breath and inhale the confidence, and exhale any self-doubt.

Now, I know you may be thinking, "Well, Sylvester, I'm just not that confident. What can I do to help build up my confidence?" My friend, you are in luck. You will receive a confidence boost in your, Manifest Greatness assessment at the end of the chapter. I want you to take out a piece of paper, and at the top of that paper, I want you to write "Brag Sheet." Now, this is not an activity to create arrogance. This is about helping you to build your self-confidence. I know you have done something in your life where you: Overcame an obstacle or accomplished something, big or small. We need to recognize those things. Sometimes we can have a hard time remembering our past successes. So I want you to take time and reflect on your previous wins?

On this Brag Sheet, I want you to write down three things that you have accomplished or examples where you have experienced success. If there is ever a moment where you are struggling with dealing with being confident, I want you to pull that Brag Sheet out and take a look at it, and say "I am powerful. I am confident." You can use your Brag Sheet to help build the confidence in yourself so that you can manifest the greatness that is inside of you.

MANIFEST GREATNESS ASSESSMENT 2
IMPROVE SELF-CONFIDENCE

<u>PERSONAL BRAG SHEET</u>

WHAT ARE 3 THINGS YOU ARE PROUD TO HAVE ACHIEVED OR OVERCOME IN YOUR LIFE?

1)

2)

3)

3

CONSISTENCY

MANIFEST GREATNESS

WE ARE WHAT WE REPEATEDLY DO.

EXCELLENCE THEN, IS NOT AN ACT BUT A HABIT.

—

-ARISTOTLE-

MANIFESTGREATNESS.ORG

The famous martial artist and philosopher, Bruce Lee once said, "Long-term consistency, trumps short-term intensity."

For us to reach the goals that we desire, we need to be consistent in our actions. What we do every day is most important, not what we occasionally do. I want to share a story that exemplifies this point of how consistency truly can help you to be successful in the long haul. The story is about two world-class explorers who were trying to be the first to make it to the South Pole. You had Mr.

Roald Amundsen, and you had Mr. Robert Falcon Scott.

Now, if you were trying to reach the South Pole, how would you go about it? Would you hike 40 miles in one day, 60 the next, and when the weather was terrible, take a break and rest? Or would you be consistent and plan to travel 20 miles every single day. If the weather is terrible, we will still hike 20 miles. If the weather conditions are excellent, we will stick to the plan and still only hike 20 miles.

A consistent 20 Mile March is what Mr. Amundsen chose. The other explorer Mr. Scott and his team decided a different path one that was inconsistent and sporadic. When the weather was great, then they would hike longer. When the weather was not great, they would rest or go a shorter distance.

So who made the right decision Mr. Scott or Mr. Amundsen? What ended up happening, the path of consistency paid off. The 20 Mile March paid off. Mr. Amundsen and his team made it to the South

Pole first. So when Mr. Scott made it 35 days later, he was welcomed with the Norwegian flag planted in the ground that Mr. Amundsen and his team had left behind in triumph. The ending to this story is very tragic, Mr. Scott and his team, never made it home safely. On their way back from the South Pole they perished only 11 miles from the next rest stop. The moral of the story is, consistency wins. I want you to ask yourself, what does your 20 Mile March look like toward reaching your goal and manifesting greatness. You must believe

consistency indeed is the friend of the great ones.
Be consistent.

Manifest Greatness Assessment 3
CREATE YOUR 20 MILE MARCH PLAN

Use the principles below to craft your personal 20-Mile March to help achieve your goal. Keep in mind your 20-Mile March should be aligned with your personality and environment conditions. What worked for one person may not be the plan for you. Also what worked for you at a different time in life may not work for you today. Be honest with yourself. Find a pace for you that you can achieve on a consistent basis.

What action(s) will you take consistently to achieve your goal?

What are the clear performance markers?

What are the self-imposed constraints?

Is this realistic?

Are the actions required mostly within your control?

What is a realistic timeframe?
(Not too long but not too short)

When will you start?

Can this be achieved with high consistency in behavior?

4

SACRIFICE

MANIFEST GREATNESS

THERE IS
NO SUCCESS
WITHOUT
SACRIFICE

—

MANIFESTGREATNESS.ORG

I want to share with you about the critical role sacrifice plays in manifesting greatness. It is something that plays a part in every journey to success. There is a direct correlation between how much success you have and how much you will have to sacrifice to get there. As you journey on your road to greatness, you have to know that the greater success you desire, the greater the sacrifice that will be required. So, what does this all mean?

The person who wishes to accomplish only very little, they do not need to sacrifice very much. The person who wants to achieve a respectable amount will have to sacrifice more. Now those of us on Team Greatness who have dreams of changing the world, we need to be willing to sacrifice more than most. So, that may mean less free time; fewer hours of binge-watching Netflix; you may be unable to party as much. Are you ready to do what the great leaders of the world have done? You will need to spend your time focused on more productive activities.

Where focus goes, energy grows. You do not just wake up, and all of a sudden and you are Floyd Mayweather a 50-0 undefeated world champion boxer, or Steph Curry, NBA champion. You do not just wake up and you are a world renowned radiologist like Dr. Laveil Allen. You do not just wake up and you are a successful fashion entrepreneur like Shevare' Perry. It does not just happen that way, a sacrifice is required. The people whose success that you admire made sacrifices to get there.

I want to share a beautiful story that highlights the level of sacrifice that is needed to manifest greatness I saw while watching the 2016 Summer Olympics. One of the races I was excited to see was the 400 meter women's finals. Before the race the announcers made a big deal of two premier runners on the track, Miss Shaunae Miller from the Bahamas and Miss Allyson Felix from the United States. On your mark, set, POW the gun went off and all 8 contenders took off from the start line with great enthusiasm. They were running hard and as expected it was a close race through the first

300 meters. As they rounded the corner approaching the final hundred meters Felix and Miller were neck and neck. When they got to the last five meters they were both giving it all they had running stride for stride. At the finish line Miss Shaunae Miller she chose to sacrifice even more and dove across the finish line running full speed and scraping her body as she landed on the track. What happened? She won by .07 seconds. Point 07 seconds was the difference between manifesting greatness for the gold and the silver medal. I have so much love for both athletes

however, diving across that finish line was the ultimate sacrifice that made the difference. This was an excellent example for all of us on Team Greatness.

Ask yourself are you diving across the finish line to manifest your greatness? Only you know if you are, but it is an easy self-check question that you can ask yourself. Are you really going that hard? Are you willing to make the sacrifices that are necessary to make things happen with the same intensity of Olympic Gold Medalist, Shaunae Miller?

On a final note if you are not willing to make the sacrifices your goals require please know you are making a different sacrifice. The sacrifice that you are making instead is your goal. You are choosing to sacrifice the greatness; you are choosing to forgo the dream instead of sacrificing some distraction to do what it takes to Manifest Greatness. Dive across the finish line.

Manifest Greatness Assessment 4

Improve Focus and Reduce Distractions

SACRIFICE FOR GREATNESS

List 5 distractions you are willing to sacrifice for greatness?

1)

2)

3)

4)

5)

POWER

OF

FIVE

MANIFEST GREATNESS

THINKING ALONE IS NOT ENOUGH. TAKE ACTION!

I want to share with you about execution. Ultimately, it is about getting things done. When you have a goal you must put action behind it to make great things happen. In this world there are a ton of great ideas that people think up every single day. However, what the world needs is more ideas done. That is where you come in. Ideas done, is what I like to define as innovation. The idea itself cannot stand alone it needs the action and that action requires your execution. So what stands in your way of executing? It is the thing that holds most people back from manifesting greatness.

However, the great ones conquer it. That thing you will overcome is called procrastination. Our failure to self-regulate causes us not to take action on our goals and the things we believe are important. Procrastination is the art of keeping up with yesterday, and we are not trying to do that. Our goal is to get meaningful things done; we are here on this Earth to Manifest Greatness.

One of the most productive American Presidents was, Dwight D. Eisenhower. He felt that people should spend their time on what was truly important to them. Those are the tasks that fall into Quadrant 1 and Quadrant 2 of the, Eisenhower Matrix.

(See Diagram On Next Page)

The Eisenhower Matrix

	Urgent	Not Urgent
Important	**Quadrant 1** Important and Urgent	**Quadrant 2** Important but Not Urgent
Not Important	**Quadrant 3** Urgent But Not Important	**Quadrant 4** Not Important And Not Urgent

Unfortunately, the person who is not productive spends too much time in Quadrant 3 and 4. He only comes to Quadrant 1 when he is very close to a deadline or either when it is too late. However, we want to dedicate more time to Quadrant 2 on things that are important but not urgent. Here is where we stretch ourselves and achieve breakthrough moments. We Manifest Greatness in Quadrant 2.

So how do you conquer procrastination and create a culture of execution that allows you to spend more time in quadrant 2? The solution is the Power Of 5. This is a principle that I live by. The Power Of 5 is a topic that I talk about when I deliver keynotes for companies, universities, or organizations. It is the difference between surviving and thriving.

It is a very simple philosophy, do five things a day toward reaching your goal, no matter how big or how small they are. I repeat, do five things a day toward achieving your goal, no matter how big or how small they are.

What happens when you do that? The desired outcome is the creation of a body of work all centered around achieving one goal. Imagine if you do five things today and let's just say you only do it 5 days a week. That is 5 times 5, that is 25 things a week that you have done all focused on your goal. It does not matter how big or small they are. The point is for you to create a habit of taking massive action on things that are important to you. The Power Of 5 will enhance your 20-Mile March.

I will use myself as an example. One goal that I have is to get my books and online courses in the hands of people worldwide who desire to learn how to live without limits. I believe it is a noble cause. So what action can I take to create this reality? One, a very simple way: I could just send a tweet and say, "Hey entrepreneurs I'm here! #entrepreneurship." It is small; however, it is still progress toward reaching my goal. So it counts.

A second thing could be something more significant. It could be giving a speaking engagement, or it could be consulting with a company; or it could be talking to a coaching client; or it could be making a new, Manifest Greatness video.

The point is, you do 5 things every single day toward reaching your goal no matter how small or how big they are. So then what happens? You end up creating a body of work all centered around one goal. So think about the goal that you have right now, something that you are working on, something that you could be struggling to get off the ground. Ask yourself what action can you take today?

This really can help the creatives or my friends in the startup world who suffer from what I like to call, "entrepreneurial paralysis." It can be a tough space to navigate and you can get stuck at some point. But this is about helping you create progress and help keep that momentum going toward reaching your goal.

As you continue to make The Power Of 5 part of your new daily rituals, your focused effort on that one goal, will produce positive results. If you have been waiting on permission to start living your best life, let me help. You have permission. Take action.

Manifest Greatness Assessment 5

Increase Performance On Goals

Use your, "Power Of 5 Journal" to track your progress on your goal. Download a free week at the link below to get started on your goal.

Be Great!

www.sylvesterchisom.com/powerof5

6

MAXIMIZE YOUR RESOURCES

MANIFEST GREATNESS

YOU DON'T LACK RESOURCES YOU LACK RESOURCEFULNESS

—

-TONY ROBBINS-

MANIFESTGREATNESS.ORG

I want to share with you about maximizing your resources. A huge part of success is utilizing everything that you are able to access. Ask yourself the following question. Am I really taking advantage of all of the resources that I have available to me? If I had asked Sylvester Stallone that question, when he was making Rocky One he would say yes.

What If I told you, you had a million dollars and 28 days to make a major box office hit, what kind of film would you make? What movie would you make?

Well, that is exactly what happened with my man, Sylvester Stallone when he wanted to make the movie he wrote, "Rocky 1." They gave him a $1,075,000 production budget and 28 days to shoot the movie. So, that shows you the studio did not really believe in his goal of creating his movie. To make it even worse with only $106 in his bank account he had already turned down $300,000 for the rights to the movie. That shows you how much confidence Stallone had in himself. He was determined to make the film on his terms. Stallone took that million dollars and that 28 days and said lets Manifest Greatness. That is all he had access to and he said you know what, "I am going to prove my greatness, I am going to show them how amazing this movie is going to be so that I really can get a big budget the next time around." So, with that million dollars and that 28 days he made "Rocky 1." In 1976, "Rocky won three Academy Awards, including Best Picture. Stallone recalled, "Literally, I was parking cars 10 months earlier and now here we are at the Oscars."

Fast forward, the six film, "Rocky" franchise has taken in more than a billion dollars at the box office since 1976. Six Rocky movies later it is easy to say that they should have given Sylvester Stallone more money to make the first movie. But, he did what he had to do with what he had. He believed in himself and he was resourceful.

You have to take advantage of what you have available to you right now. So, I know you may have big goals, big dreams, big career ideas that you are working on. You may have a million-dollar business idea but to be honest it probably does not take that to get started. The thing to do is to get started with what you have access to right now, be resourceful and manifest that greatness with what you have.

My childhood friend and business partner, Arthur and I started our first business, Showroom Shine when we were 17, with only a water hose, a bucket and a dream. We had to be very resourceful in the early days. We have had a lot of success with that business. We learned a lot of valuable business lessons at a young age. We have grown it into a company with multiple locations and Fortune 500 corporate partnerships. I like to use the water hose and bucket from my story as a motivating metaphor for others. Ask yourself what is your water hose and bucket? What resources do you have access to now that can help you get started?

There are so many great success stories that have small beginnings and resourceful founders. Steve Jobs started Apple in his parents' garage, and the first Disney Studio was in a one car garage in the back of Walt Disney's uncle's house.

Here is something that you have to ask yourself. What's stopping you? What resources do you have available to you right now and how can you take full advantage of those? Create your, "Rocky." The most important resource you need to develop is your resourcefulness.

Manifest Greatness Assessment 6

Improve Resourcefulness

Write down one hurdle that stands in the way of you achieving your goal.

Brainstorm and write down five possible solutions to overcoming your hurdle.

1)

2)

3)

4)

5)

7

CRAFT

YOUR

ENVIRONMENT

MANIFEST GREATNESS

COLLABORATE WITH PEOPLE YOU CAN LEARN FROM

-PHARRELL-

MANIFESTGREATNESS.ORG

UNLOCK

SECRET

CHAPTER

Visit:
sylvesterchisom.com/seven

PASSWORD: TEAMGREATNESS

(MUST BE IN ALL CAPS)

Manifest Greatness Assessment 7

Improve your network

Reach out to 3 people who have helped you on your journey and tell them thank you for something they have done to help you.

Find 3 people who have achieved the goal you are working toward or something similar. Reach out to them for a meeting or research their pathway to success. LinkedIn or Google search may help you find these people.

Find 3 places that you can visit that could help you achieve your goal and schedule time to go there. This could be a meetup, conference, networking event, or just a cool place that provides inspiration.

Search online for 3 pieces of content that will give you more information or inspiration to reach your goal. This could be a blog, article, or YouTube video.

8

WALK
IN
YOUR
TRUTH

MANIFEST GREATNESS

BE CONGRUENT,
BE AUTHENTIC,
BE YOUR
TRUE SELF.

—

-GANDHI-

MANIFESTGREATNESS.ORG

82

When you hear the words walking in your truth, what comes to mind for you? For me I think about having an unwavering commitment to the vision of the life you desire for yourself. I believe the commitment has to be unwavering because everyone may not fully understand the value of your pursuit.

I want to share with you the backstory of FedEx and the founder Fred Smith. I like to highlight him whenever I am talking to people about the entrepreneurial mindset and walking in your truth.

While Fred was attending college at Yale he wrote a paper on the concept of FedEx. We all know today of the value that his company adds to the world. However, as the story goes his professor did not understand the vision and gave Fred a failing grade. It is almost unimaginable in today's time that he did not receive an A on his paper.

What if he quit on his idea because his professor did not believe in him? He would have stopped short of living his truth and helping all of us receive our Amazon packages in the mail. Fred's commitment was unwavering.

Think about how many times you have shared your idea with someone and only for them to stomp on it. They break it down. They tell you every reason why it will not work. Every reason why you are not the person to fulfill that mission. They tell you why there is no way that you can manifest greatness in that endeavor. That is not your truth.

That is someone else's lie. That is where your passion can come into play. Your passion will help you to have an unwavering belief that what you are working on you will eventually develop mastery level skills. You must believe that your truth is worthy of your time and your energy.

I recently heard a story about the American film producer Tyler Perry, his movies have grossed nearly a billion dollars. When he was young he had dreams of being a famous playwright and movie producer. However, when he first started the plays he produced were not well attended or financially successful. To go even deeper when Tyler first launched his now famous, "Madea" character he was homeless and lived in his car, but he did not give up on his dream.

What did he do? He boldly walked in his truth. He kept pushing through the sacrifice to create successful plays, television shows, and box office hits. That is what it takes to live your truth. You cannot allow other people to distract or deter you from giving your time and energy to a worthwhile pursuit when you know that your destiny is to manifest greatness in that space. You must take action. That is your mission. Everyone is not going to understand that. It is important to accept that it is not meant for everyone to understand because the truth belongs to you and no one else. You cannot live small in fear of what other people may think of you taking action on your dreams and passions.

The final part to help you walk in your truth is understanding the power of patience. You have to run your race. Do not compare your chapter one to someone else's chapter ten. Dwayne "The Rock" Johnson says it best, "Success isn't overnight. It's when every day you get a little better than the day before. It all adds up."

There are no shortcuts to get there. Consistent and focused hard work will allow you to continue to write great chapters of success in your book. As a professional speaker, I am often asked by other new speakers how do I get to do Ted Talks, speak to Fortune 100 companies, universities and major conferences across the world. I tell them the key is serving with an attitude of gratitude. I tell them you have to appreciate and honor the smaller opportunities before you are offered the larger events. There is a level of sacrifice that you will have to make. It is easy to see someone else further along in their career and become envious. Try to remember you do not know the sacrifices that those people or someone else has made on their behalf. Focus on your path. Your walk just may take a little longer.

I remember when my business partner and I were in Atlanta and we were invited to sit in on the Steve Harvey Radio show. We were there the Monday after he was on the *Oprah Winfrey Show* for the first time. He was still riding the high of his first book, "*Act Like a Lady, Think Like a Man.*" He was so excited. It would be so easy to say in that moment wow everything is coming so easy to him. But I had to remind myself Steve has 30 years on us as an entrepreneur walking in his truth.

When they went off the air, I remember him telling us a story about his journey. Steve said he could remember driving to some little town for a small amount of money to do a comedy show. He said when he got there, he was like, where is the stage? When it was time for him to go on for his set in the middle of the bar of this little town, they threw out a milk crate and said, "There's your stage." He got on that stage and he told those jokes like he was in front of 20,000. Fast forward to the current moment. It is a normal occurrence for him to be seen by millions on his television shows every week and to perform in large arenas and venues. Who knows how much he got paid in that small bar years ago but now if you want to book Steve Harvey, you are lucky if he agrees and be ready to pay a price that a legend deserves.

If you are another comedian, you cannot compare your chapter two or three to his chapter 25 now. There are levels to greatness. Along those levels you get better with time. You have to respect the levels.

As long as you are working toward your goal and you are serving others with your gifts know that you are walking in your truth.

Manifest Greatness Assessment 8

Visualize Your Goal

1. Close your eyes and visualize yourself walking in your truth.

    What are you doing?
    What do you see?
    Who is with you?
    How do you feel?

    Take a deep inhale and slowly exhale, use your breath to give
    energy to your image. You are filling your goal with positive
    energy and intention. Repeat this five times.

2. Once, you have completed step one close your eyes again and
    consider what steps you will take over the next few days to move
    you closer to your goal. Feel free to refer back to your 20-mile
    march.

9

GRATITUDE

GRATITUDE UNLOCKS
THE FULLNESS
OF LIFE

There are two things that can stop all of us from manifesting greatness. If you conquer these two things, you will step into that next level of success for yourself. You will have an easier journey in going from ordinary to extraordinary. The two things that we need to conquer are anger and fear. These are the two things that I feel can hold you back in the greatest way. The goal is to get to the other side of anger and fear.

What you will find on the other side is gratitude. The great ones understand this principle. Where you find gratitude you will find happiness. Ultimately I want you to have an extreme level of joy with your family, school, work, and your lifestyle. The great ones are happy and experience an abundance of gratitude. They show more gratitude, and that is because they have been able to conquer both anger and fear.

I want you to think about something as it relates to fear. How many times have you wanted to talk to someone and you just didn't pick up the telephone and make the call? Or why didn't you just send an email you should have sent? Why didn't you go and say hello when that person was in the room? Why didn't you go and introduce yourself? Why didn't you ask for what you wanted? Did you make an excuse like I need more time, or something wasn't right? Why didn't you apologize first? Be honest, were you were afraid?

Here is a wonderful strategy that will help you push beyond that fear next time. I learned this, from one of my virtual mentors Tony Robbins.

He talked about a routine that he does to get himself psyched up and in the position to show more gratitude. He said every day he primes himself. It is not a quiet meditation type of thing. It is an active meditation. You can actually watch him doing it on his Netflix original movie, "I Am Not Your Guru."

Tony said every morning he gives himself about 10 minutes to do this. First he does three sets of 30 breaths. It is high intensity breathing where he is breathing in deep and then pushing it out his nose.

The reason why he said he does it that way is because your breath is like the string on a kite. The string is the breath, and the kite is your brain. When you try this, it will elevate the way you think. It will change the way you feel. You are changing your state by doing this breathing.

Secondly, Tony will take three minutes to focus on three moments that he is grateful for. Try to focus on three moments that you are grateful for. Do not lightly think about those moments, but try to go deep into those moments. Close your eyes and really feel those moments. Try to remember the colors or the sounds or smells from those moments. Truly feel three things you are grateful for. That could be your family. That could be an experience. That could be your work. It could be anything but visualize those moments.

Thirdly, focus on three people who you are grateful for, and think about why you are grateful for them in your life. What are your experiences like with those people?

Finally, to push you further and closer to manifesting your greatness, think of three things that you intend on accomplishing. As you think about that really try to visualize those moments of accomplishment. What does it feel like experiencing that accomplishment? Doing this changes what happens in your brain. You cannot physically experience it yet, but you can visualize yourself having those accomplishments.

When you do these exercises it changes the way you approach the world. You are now better prepared to take on anger and fear and not allow them to be your distractions. Instead, you conquer them with an intense focus on changing your state to one of gratitude.

Manifest Greatness Assessment 9

State Change

Read Tony Robbins morning state change activity. Give it a try when you wake up tomorrow and see if it helps you approach the day with greater focus and intensity on gratitude. Write down your results.

10

LAW

OF

VALUE

MANIFEST GREATNESS

ONLY A LIFE LIVED FOR OTHERS IS WORTH LIVING

———

-ALBERT EINSTEIN-

MANIFESTGREATNESS.ORG

"Only a life lived for others is worth living."

I think these words represent and connect deeply with the principle of adding value. To manifest greatness, you must continuously add value in all your relationships and interactions with other people.

If you always add value, you will remain employed. You will rise to the top of organizations or companies. You will be a leader in your industry, a leader in your family, and a leader amongst your friends.

A great example of a person who manifests greatness in this way is one of my mentors, Jeff Hoffman. Jeff Hoffman is a global advocate for entrepreneurship, education, and is one of the co-founders of Priceline. He is a very successful entrepreneur with many companies under his belt. Now, he spends much of his time traveling the world talking to youth about success through entrepreneurship.

I have had the pleasure of sharing the stage with him at a couple of different conferences.

Most recently we were both speaking at a conference in Kansas City. We were staying in the same hotel. There were several other dynamic speakers in town. On the last night of the conference after my friend, Felecia Hatcher delivered the closing keynote we all decided to go to dinner.

Before we went to dinner, I was waiting for my friends in the lobby. Jeff so happened to be in the lobby at the same time and he was asking the concierge what's a great place to have barbeque in

Kansas City? They told him a restaurant that was far away. Me being from St. Louis and having a connection with the Gates BBQ family, I suggested that he go to Gates BBQ. I said, you are in Kansas City. If you have never gone to Gates, you should go there. It is classic Kansas City barbeque. Jeff took my advice and headed there for dinner.

My friends finally came down, and they wanted BBQ too. So we ended up going to Gates BBQ. As we left I told them there was a chance that we may run into Jeff there. So, we make it there and get our barbeque. As we walk to our seat sure enough, he is sitting at a table not too far away from us.

We are sitting at a table, and here at our table, you have four of the top speakers in the nation. It so happens all of us are African-American sitting at this table. We were eating, laughing, and talking about how the conference went.

Jeff had finished his meal and was preparing to leave. Being the awesome human and giving person that he is; He comes by and says, "You guys are awesome. Great job today at the conference. It was a pleasure meeting all of you. You mind if I pull up a chair?"

So, he pulls up a chair. Now we thought he would stay for maybe a few minutes to small talk. Next thing you know, he is sharing stories and strategies for entrepreneurship and international business. He is giving us insight into all these different companies that he has worked with and his philosophy on starting a business and what it takes to be successful. We look up, an hour passes. Two hours pass. He is telling us stories about being on Richard Branson's island and spending time with the family that owns Volkswagen and all of these billionaire entrepreneur stories that are truly priceless. He did not have to do that, but it was important to him to not miss that moment. He took that opportunity to add value to what he saw as four high-potential entrepreneurs who he wanted to advise. He added so much value to our businesses that evening and gave us great stories to share with others around the world.

That is the same approach you want to have. You never want to miss a moment to add value. We left that restaurant when it closed. We literally shut it down. As we drove back to the hotel in the car we were all like, wow. That was a moment. We just had a moment here in Kansas City that we will never forget, having BBQ with a billionaire. That is what happens when you add value. You touch people and inspire people in a way that is remarkable, memorable, and impactful.

When you do that, the law of reciprocity will work for you. Positive people, energy, and experiences will be added to your life and you will manifest greatness. Add value everywhere you go.

Manifest Greatness Assessment 10

Add Value

1) How do you feel when you add value to others?

2) What are some ways that you currently add value to others?

3) How can you take the next step up and add more value to other people?

11

OPRAH

SUCCESS

FORMULA

MANIFEST GREATNESS

IF YOU WANT YOUR LIFE TO BE MORE REWARDING YOU HAVE TO CHANGE THE WAY YOU THINK.

-OPRAH-

MANIFESTGREATNESS.ORG

I believe you will make a great impact on the world. Sometimes, we see successful people and we wonder, how did they get to that point? How did they achieve so much? I will never forget, I heard an interview with Oprah, and they were asking her, Oprah, what makes you different?

She said, my philosophy is simple. I want to give all of myself to the world. All of my gifts, all of my talents, I want to give all of that to the world. I was in awe of her response. For me, I found that answer profound in understanding and defining true greatness and success. Everyone in the world can do something greater to utilize their personal gifts and talents better. You were born with a different set of gifts, skills, talents, different life experiences from anyone else. Your uniqueness is valuable and you should offer it back to the community, give it to the world.

After hearing Oprah's success formula, I took time and reflected on my gifts and talents that I have to offer the world. For me that ended up expressing itself in a book, *The Young Entrepreneur's Guide to Success 2.0.* It was my second book, and it has been a beautiful journey ever since. I took all of my life experiences as a successful young entrepreneur and tried to turn it into something where I get a chance to teach and inspire the next generation of entrepreneurs and people who want to overcome their limiting beliefs.

That book and online curriculum are used in school districts all across the country. Every year I am invited to speak at high schools, colleges, corporations, and conferences all across the country about the entrepreneurial mindset.

I want to tell you a quick personal story about the impact you can make when you give your gift to the world. You never know how what you are doing can impact someone else. I was in Delaware for a series of keynotes, and they told me that they were using my book in a community re-entry program in the Delaware prison system for men and women. They use my book to show how entrepreneurship can be a promising career choice for them to take care of their families and to empower them to think about taking ownership over their own lives. I would never have thought my books or my gifts would have such an impact and be able to help others in this way.

So just imagine how your gifts and talents can impact the world. I challenge you to be like Oprah. Give all of yourself to the world and manifest greatness.

Manifest Greatness Assessment 11

Utilize Your Gifts

1) Write down one example where you used your gifts or talents to help someone else?

2) How can you better use your gifts, talents, and life experiences to make a greater impact on the world?

12

LIMITLESS SUCCESS

MANIFEST GREATNESS

ALL
LIMITS
ARE
SELF IMPOSED

—

-ICARUS-

MANIFESTGREATNESS.ORG

128

I want to share with you about limitless success. This principle will tap the core of your belief system. I want you to know the only limits that exist are the ones you place on yourself. This is very important so I will repeat it. The only limits that exist for you are the ones that you place on yourself. You have to know that your circumstances do not limit you. You are not limited by what part of town you come from. You are not limited by who your parents are. You are not limited by: You being the first one to graduate high school, go to college, graduate college. You are not limited by you being the first one to live in a good neighborhood. If you are the first one to break any of these barriers, you do not have to limit yourself with any of these things. If you come from a family without money do not let that limit you. Even on the success side. If you come from a family with money, you are not limited by it. If you are a male, if you are a female; if you live an alternative lifestyle; if you are the first to learn English; none of these situations limit you. The only limits that exist are the ones you place on yourself. The premise of this book is centered around you overcoming any limiting beliefs.

I want to share a quick story with you about a conversation I had with business titan, David Steward on limits. Dave Steward is the founder of Worldwide Technology. It is the largest black-owned company in the country. They do over $9 billion in annual revenue and is ranked 28 on Fortune's 100 Best Companies to Work list.

Mr. Steward was talking and he was telling his story about how he was at one of the oldest banks on Wall Street and the CEO was giving him a tour. Mr. Steward said it just hit him to ask the CEO, how much money exchanges hands at the bank on a daily basis? The CEO told him over a trillion dollars a day exchanges hands at the bank. Mr. Steward said to me, "Sylvester that answer made me believe, I'm thinking too small. I need to ask myself, what percentage of those transactions do I want to be mine?"

Keep in mind this is someone who is already running a multibillion-dollar company and one of the greatest places to work for in America. Now, if a person like that can believe there is still room to grow and that there are no limits, you should model this same behavior. Dave Steward is taking the limits off his thinking in terms of the impact that he can make in the world with his company and philanthropic activities.

There is room for all of us to push forward and remove the limits from our gifts and talents.

To live with a limitless mindset, you have to work on your belief system. You have to first believe that you can run a multimillion dollar company if that is your desire. You also have to believe you can run a multibillion dollar business if that is your desire. They both will require you to remove limiting beliefs. Your dreams and goals must be infused with a limitless mindset.

It really comes down to your belief system. What story are you telling yourself? Your story is one of resilience and power. Greatness in, Greatness out!

Manifest Greatness Assessment 12

Remove Limiting Beliefs

What limiting beliefs may be holding you back from greatness?

Write down the new required beliefs in order to manifest greatness and accomplish your goal?

Write down 5 positive statements about yourself starting with the words, "I am." Repeat each statement out loud 5 times. Take a photo of these and refer to them in moments of self- doubt.

I am _____

I am _____

I am _____

I am _____

I am _____

13

SHIP IT!

MANIFEST GREATNESS

THERE IS NO
SHORTAGE OF
REMARKABLE
IDEAS.
WHAT'S MISSING
IS THE WILL TO
EXECUTE THEM.

-SETH GODIN-

MANIFESTGREATNESS.ORG

138

This is the final principle to help you achieve your next breakthrough. Recently, I was delivering a keynote at a conference in Denver, and while at dinner a good friend and business partner John called me. John is the founder of the ed-tech startup, Real World Scholars. He was so energized and pumped about his new idea. It was a very inspirational message for me, and I just wanted to share it with you.

John explained to me about what he had been studying lately. His research was on how we can help get more ideas out into the world. He expressed to me that is what we should be measuring and focusing our attention on. The point of it was, ship it. John went on, ship it. Ship it! Ship it! Sylvester. Ship it! I'm like, what do you mean?

He starts explaining it and shared a Steve Jobs quote with me. "You are never more than one great idea away from achieving a major breakthrough. It's entirely possible that you have already had the breakthrough idea, but you will not see the breakthrough until you ship it." Creative thinking should be followed by creative doing. Give your idea, answer, or insight the opportunity to live outside of your imagination and notes."

-Steve Jobs

It is incredible to know that you are only one idea away from your next breakthrough. The crazy part about it is you may already have that idea. You may be sitting on that idea. That idea may be written in an old journal. You may have just talked about it with a friend. If you are anything like me, it is something that is keeping you up at night. The problem is you have not shipped the idea. You have to get the idea out. There is no shortage of great ideas; we need ideas done.

Put more emphasis on shipping your ideas and getting them out into the world if you want to achieve those breakthrough moments. What are you waiting on?

I recently witnessed a great story about shipping your idea. On HBO's, "The Defiant One's" a documentary about Dr. Dre and Jimmy Iovine they shared the story of how they came up with the idea for Beats By Dre headphones. Dr. Dre and Jimmy Iovine have neighboring beach homes. One day Dre is standing on his balcony overlooking the ocean, and Jimmy so happens to be walking down the beach at the same time. Jimmy yells to Dre, "Hey I'm coming up."

Jimmy comes up and Dre starts to tell Jimmy that his lawyer approached him to endorse a sneaker company. Dre was explaining to Jimmy that he told his lawyer no because he wears the same pair of sneakers every day and does not consider himself to be the most fashionable guy. Jimmy agreed and told Dre, "You shouldn't do sneakers you should do speakers! All types of speakers and headphones."

Dre thought it was a good idea and said, "Yea we could call them Beats." Dr. Dre said the conversation was no more than ten minutes if that. Jimmy left Dre's balcony and continued on his stroll down the beach. A few days later Jimmy called Dr. Dre to his office and had 100 different headphones on the table to start comparing what they liked and did not like about what was currently on the market. From that casual conversation, "Beats By Dre" was born. They shipped the idea and eventually sold it to Apple for $3.2 billion.

How many conversations like that have you had where a great idea was born but no one followed up with action? There is no reason to keep waiting. If you have some idea that can help other people or that can make an impact on the world, it is essential that you work hard to ship it. I believe shipping ideas is a key measurement tool that we should use in terms of thinking about success. Truly, let's get these ideas out. If you are sitting on an idea right now, I put an acronym together to encourage you to launch. When you think of S.H.I.P, I want you to think of Start Here, It's Possible. Start Here, It's Possible. Dr. Dre and Jimmy Iovine did it and so can you. Take more action on your ideas.

Manifest Greatness Assessment 13

Increase Execution Speed

What ideas have you shipped so far toward reaching your goal?

What actions can you take to start shipping your ideas faster without reducing the quality of your work?

A Message From The Author

"Manifest Greatness," truly came from my heart. I am here to help you take action on your dreams with your gifts. My desire was for this book to help you push past any limiting beliefs that are holding you back. All of these principles represent the entrepreneurial mindset. I am a firm believer that all 21st century leaders will benefit from understanding and applying the principles outlined in Manifest Greatness. I would love to hear your thoughts on this book and how it has impacted your way of thinking and living.

s a daily pursuit to Manifest Greatness. What
practice in private you will later be rewarded
n public. To help you focus I have created
inspirational reminders: Free weekly videos,
iews, hats, shirts, memes, and so much more.
out the website and connect on social media
re great content. Remember you don't have
reat to get started, but you have to get
to be great. So, continue to ship those ideas
NIFEST GREATNESS. It is a lifestyle.

ter Chisom

GET THE GEAR!

There are hints
about **who
you are**
in what you wear.

There are **hints** about
who you are
in **what you wear.**

BOOK YOUR NEXT SPEAKER

WATCH SYLVESTER'S TED TALK AT
SYLVESTERCHISOM.COM/SPEAKING

LET'S GET SOCIAL

 @mrchisom

 @sylvesterchisom

 @sylvesterchisom

 youtube.com/
sylvesterchisom

 @mrchisom

manifestgreatness.org

MANIFEST GREATNESS

"MANIFEST GREATNESS PODCAST"

ANCHOR.FM/MANIFESTGREATNESS.ORG

About The Author

Sylvester Chisom, is an education technology entrepreneur. He is the author of three books and online courses. His previous book is entitled, "The Young Entrepreneurs' Guide To Success 2.0."

Sylvester Chisom has been recognized as one of Ebony Magazine's Top Young Entrepreneurs. He started his entrepreneurial journey at the age of 17, founding the Steve Harvey Neighborhood Award winning Showroom Shine Express Detailing. He has earned a reputation as a leading authority on motivating people to success through the application of the entrepreneurial mindset. His books and online courses are used in school districts, colleges, and companies across the country. Sylvester keeps a busy schedule as a keynote speaker and consultant for companies and schools.

He has been featured in The Wall Street Journal, INC Magazine, The Steve Harvey Morning Show, and more. Learn more about his work and how you can inspire those around you at **ManifestGreatness.org**

Sylvester's Favorite Cause

The Show Me Costa Rica Project is Sylvester's favorite organization to give his time. They offer premium coffee for the premium cause of sending inner city students on an international education trip to Costa Rica. So far they have sent 82 students to Costa Rica and raised over $200,000 for the cause. Learn more at **showmecostaricacoffee.com**

If this book inspired you,

please pass it on to someone you want to inspire.

-Sylvester Chisom

Manifestgreatness.org